Ann Phillips lives in Frome, Somerset, is married with two children and three grandchildren. Ann is a trained Spiritual Director and a Church of England Lay Reader in Holy Trinity Church, Frome.

Ann sees in her family history the two strands of Army and Church running through the generations; she has been involved in both; as an Army Nursing Sister and now as an Anglican Lay Reader. Ann regularly preaches in her church and is active in many related christian concerns.

Ann has a BA in Humanities from the Open University and has recently resumed writing poetry more seriously.

Edited by Gerry Phillips,
Printed by : Inky Little Fingers Ltd.,
Churcham Business Park, Gloucester, GL2 8AX

INBETWEEN LANDS

Poems

by

Ann Phillips

Dedicated to our dear Peter and Barbara Phillips

who have been such a source of fun,

laughter and companionship through the years.

Contents

Introduction

This collection of poetry arose out of a year attending a poetry workshop and comes with my thanks for all the suggestions and encouragement I have received.

'We have only the word, but the word will do. It will do because it is true that the poem shakes the empire, that the poem heals and transforms and rescues, that the poem enters like a thief in the night and gives new life, fresh from the word and from nowhere else. There are many pressures to quiet the text, to silence this deposit of dangerous speech, to halt this outrageous practice of speaking alternative possibility. The poems, however, refuse such silence. They sound through preachers who risk beyond prose. In the act of such risk, power is released, newness evoked, God is praised.'

© *Walter Brueggemann,*
FINALLY COMES THE POET, 142.
reprinted with permission of Augsburg Fortress Press.

Ann Phillips
Frome, 2018

The In-Between Lands

*Homage to Christian Hook the artist
and Fabrice Muamba the footballer.*

This man stands proud, poised.
Ebony face composed.
He holds the keys of the kingdom, a cross and his ball.
Converging miracles combined to give this man
a second chance.

The artist depicts time and motion in a study
of the fractured moments of the man.
He collapsed on pitch.
Cardiac arrest.
Silence fell as thousands held their breath
willing that heart to beat again.

Returned to life we see past and present collide
giving different perspectives
which illuminate the strength in his face.
The strength of his faith.

His in-between moments are captured
through layers of transparent paint.
Fractals in their complex repeating patterns are explored.
Multiple viewpoints merge with folklore and myth
to create a single image.

The artist lived and worked in the in-between lands.
Seas and oceans meeting in fierce contest,
birthing the intensity with which he approached his art.
The chaos of water hurling crashing waves' cotton-wool
spume against craggy rocks,
colours of a bleak landscape outlined
by skies' transparent light.

The Gift

From 1915 – 1917 the Ottoman Empire systematically slaughtered one and a half million Armenians. An Ottoman official called it 'the liquidation of Christian elements from society.'

It was a prosaic unpolished beginning, yet
giving a compelling account of those less fortunate
than the silver-plated privilege of the wealthy
Ottoman officials with their stamped orders.

Dismissed, forgotten, the Armenians lived on borrowed time;
one day their time ran out.
They were rounded up like animals,
caught in the curling energy and endless noise
of deliberate slaughter, hacked down and
left in barren fields and deserts
where flies feasted on their flesh.

Unspeakable atrocities endured.
The crucified, drowned, burnt.
Women and children on forced marches, flogged naked
through a desert waste of heat and thirst.
They died in their thousands.

As observer, I entered places where
death was piled on death.
Wrote words like swords that sliced the flesh from bone
then vomiting despair I turned away.
Severe depression rolled in and overtook
my blighted mind, my only comfort darkness,
the peace and quiet of night.
Still, I scribbled those haunting images
the hand curled, the eyes dulled,
the ravaged ground that cradled broken bodies.

One day I turned and saw the gift.
A yellow-bright sunflower shining
in broken pot left by some kind friend.
Then sunlight crept in through cracks and crevices
while tears flowed in release.
I could not stop, though still my mind was haunted
by those dread images,
I did go on to finalize the words
clarified in black and white.

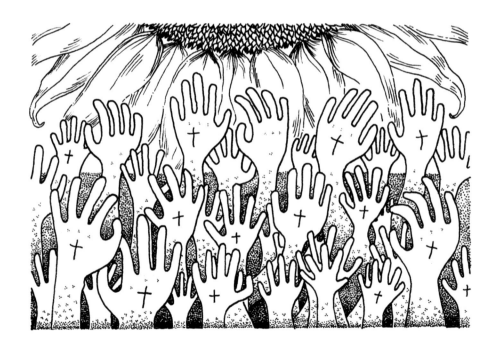

Jungle Fever

A miasma of heat rises up from jungle's growth
tread carefully there, snakes coiled round branches
can rear up with flickering tongues, and bite
their poison weaving in and through your veins.
We pause for rest, burn leeches off our legs
grown plump with our life's blood.

Thin men toiling in the sun spit blood
their lungs congested. They care not for jungle's growth
encroaching onto city roads, whip-lashing legs;
their only aim to pull on poles that branch
from rickshaws heavy weight, pumping blood through veins
that bulge with thickened walls. The dragon bites.

She ran through long grass laughing, not seeing till snake bite
stung; she cried out for someone to suck poison and blood
from her throbbing veins.
The gardener cut down all growth,
 snake bludgeoned to death. But some branches
remained, long lianas coiling round unwary legs.

The child had long tanned legs
from sunny days spent pool-side. She bites
into her sweet, swings from the branch
hanging temptingly near, falls hard and cuts pouring blood
need dressing. They drive along roads lined with exotic growth
of umbrella palms, leaves thickened with chlorophylled veins.

Smoke from joss sticks wreathed the air, insubstantial veins
of heavy incense rising through Buddha's legs.
He reclined on bamboo mat like some foreign growth,
brown arms holding her close, small love bites
marking her neck while she felt his heart pumping blood
through veins and arteries thick as tree branches.

Monkeys whoop as they swing from branch to branch
on trees lining drainage ditches, winding like veins
through Kampongs where women in sarongs, blood
red, make silken flowers and geckos clinging little legs
run up and down the walls, they do not bite.
And still the heat of jungle days brings painful growth.

She ran through darkening jungle's thick undergrowth
fear filling her heart, ignoring cuts, bruises, bites.
She disappeared long ago. The last thing we saw, tanned legs.

Cabinet of Curiosities

Travel-weary, bearing marks of wear and tear
the lady's desk still stands, though wobbly legs
are held by alien woods and nails,
an unknown geography imprinted
on its bronze handles and inset marquetry.
The rosewood cabinet sits snugly on top,
the mirrored interior containing a child's
enchanted world of jewelled caskets,
tiny glass animals, ivory Chinese figures,
a white china angel, a small stone scarab
and blown eggs painted with Russian crosses.
My eye is caught by
my father's china terrier no bigger than
two widths of my thumb, sitting
with ears cocked, a black fly on its nose,
amusement spreads a smile on my face.
I hold a moulded plastic shell that fits my palm.
 Look! within is a small world
of Chinese figures and animals standing
round a tiny mill-house, water wheel
turning in still blue stream, this was
always my favourite.

A water pot from Bethlehem made from
interwoven stalks of grain beautifully patterned,
such pots once balanced on young heads.
I see them still in those old Bible scenes though
now modernity clangs along dusty paths
where girls once trod.
A Chinese perfume bottle one of several,
this one painted on the inside with languid ladies
enjoying themselves in punts on a lake
full of water lilies. Another painted with brightly
coloured Koi carp swimming vigorously alongside
strange black script, what is it saying
and how are these wondrous small scenes of life
painted on the inside of bottles?
Another mystery, a sailing ship in full rig with
sails billowing as it glides across a blue sea,
my ship in a bottle that once rested
 in grandad's cottage.
A tortoiseshell tooth-pick holder, lid fitting
tightly across the top. Silver plaque inscribed with
John Longfellow, and on the back his family motto
'Neck or Nothing'. How did this come
 to rest in the cabinet?

A pale blue Murano glass fish from Italy, a gift

from my godmother weighs heavy

in my hand with such smooth curves.

 An ivory goddess of peace that

I brought back from Malaya hoping for

an abundance of that peace to fill

the void in my heart.

A pair of extraordinary wooden fish, carved like

mythical creatures all waving tails and fins.

An elaborate scrolled and gilded frame

enclosing a tiny photo of my grandfather.

These treasures collected through years past

by my family, hold memories

of half-forgotten stories

of people, places

and unexpected finds in foreign lands.

The Poetry of Notes

We find them in our pockets
or in a wallet, given in exchange for goods
or services that we desire.
A varied collection of colours, textures and patterns
meets our eye, both sides richly printed
with the tantalizing knowledge of secret codes
hidden within.

They have an importance for us far beyond their weight
these small pieces of paper, that fit
so neatly into our lives.
They speak of all the value we place
upon ourselves, our hopes, our dreams.
Used wisely they can change the world
or loss can drive us to despair.

She looks out at us face serene,
tiara firmly enthroned on dark hair
neatly waved, while diamonds
adorn Her Majesty. Fronting each note
the world's oldest reigning monarch has survived
thirteen prime ministers and four jubilee celebrations
since her coronation in 1953.

On five we see a pugnacious face
staring out, he lived from 1874 to 1965.
War correspondent, historian, writer and artist; a young man
who saw action in British India, Sudan and the Boer war.

Two years before his death awarded
the Nobel Prize for Literature
this iconic figure dominated
the lives and politics of a generation,
offering nothing but 'blood, toil, tears and sweat'
through long years of war.

In contrast, look at ten and here we find
a ship sailing away into sunrays while
humming bird on exotic yellow flowers
flutters wings 100 beats to the second.
A compass and magnifying glass observe
the Theory of Evolution unfold.

The man who travelled half way round the world
as biologist, scientist, geologist, no end to his
accomplishments.
Prolific writer changed our understanding of ourselves
and the natural world.

At last in Scotland's banks and braes comes twenty.
His head in profile wearing powdered wig,
his years from 1723 to 1793.
His Magnum Opus 'The Wealth of Nations'.
Numbers matter to this philosopher, but market forces
soon bring economies and devaluation.
The minor planet '12838 Adamsmith'
in memoriam.

King Offa of Mercia living 757 to 796
is responsible for the ancient origins of our currency.
He introduced the silver penny, which became
the standard coin in all Anglo-Saxon kingdoms;
240 silver pennies equal to one pound weight of silver
evolved into our modern pound sterling.

Taken for granted these familiar notes, who knows
or even thinks about their background history?
Their importance for us lies, not in their history, but
in the weight of all we receive in the exchange.

Patterns

Behind the frame threads hang loose
mixed up, crossed over, short or long
knotted or not
they dangle down, a messy throng.
Turned over, patterns are made
with weft woven through warp
bringing beauty and order out of chaos.
Textures rough or smooth, bobbly or braided,
different elements forming a story
slowly move into intricate patterns.
Smoothest velvet, rougher felt with skeins of wool
or silken thread.
Untidy piles of tangled tape
twisted.
Plastic bags cut to sharp shapes
scissored.

Colours brighten my day glowing like rubies,
sparkling like diamonds,
every shade captured.
I stroke this growing landscape
feeling, measuring, caressing the map outlined
in curves, circles, hatching, blocking or full stops.
My butterfly of threads takes flight.
While I progress through days and years
the weaver spins
my tapestry is shaped.

Past Lives

Lovely and gifted they stare out at me
Nina, Grace, Evelyn, Elinor, Estelle.
Five young women who encircle their father, the Bishop.
They arrived at Jaffa in 1887, ferried from ship to shore
through dangerous seas, wading the last few feet
weighed down by voluminous skirts.

Elinor my grandmother, seen in early photos
as a slender child, grew into a beautiful woman
with wistful eyes and an abundance of chestnut hair
which she plaited and wrapped round her head
like a coronet. She lost her only child in 1944.
I hardly knew him before he was gone.

My great aunts all left a legacy but one stands out for me:
Estelle outlived them all, a gentle presence,
hospitable and generous, her life inscribed by all the
memories of their life in Palestine.
Lonely but never alone
her faith sustained her through long days and nights.
She embraced me with love, held my first child.

Chants of prayers rise in the evening air
like incense weaving round slender spires,
a golden dome stands proud
above the city.
Through it all the Via Dolorosa winds its lonely way
and here the Man from Nazareth, bloodied by cruel thorns

and whips, dragged the crippling cross.

Now, narrow cobbled streets squashed tight
with pilgrims and tourists who pass vendors,
standing in shadowed doorways of bazaars and souks.
And men in black with high hats, long ringlets swinging
against gaunt cheeks, stride swiftly through the crowds
to unpolluted prayers.

A Time at Abbey House

Looking out --- through a window --- at Abbey ruins

    but caught in thought

by the immensity of an old oak tree,

    branches blowing in the wind

roots unseen --- holding --- rooted, grounded

    giving strength, stability.

        A window of seeing

           opened to the

             unseen.

The periphery of our lives,

the circle, the surface, that which can be seen by all ---

The unseen

    rooted and grounded in

      the reality beyond the real.

Words unable to convey

    the numinous --- the mystery

of that which is unseen --- in us

known only to God.

This hidden, unseen reality that is part of us

    yet so unrealised

that which makes you 'You' and me 'Me'

that real --- known to God

    glimpsed sometimes in us, by us;

as we meditate on that which roots and grounds us.

Or when we are still and silent before the

awesome reality

    of the living God.

Enter in --- to that mystery

    where God is waiting

for me   for you   for us.

The great I AM

    Alpha and Omega

In whom we live, we move, we have our being.

Romi at Trewartha

Following an ancient farm lane we come
to the cottage built of local stone, nestling within
encircling barns and rambling roses.

An appearance framed by the ancient wooden door,
she stands unbowed with arms outstretched
to welcome us in and time stands still.

Entering the low beamed rooms we are surrounded
by chairs, sofas, tables, every space
occupied by paintings.

Favourites are displayed, their provenance discussed,
Patrick Heron and other well-known artists mentioned;
the present is hazy but the past clear as a bell.

We take our coffee outside, empty chairs found
to rest three weary persons. Smells of mown grass and roses
seduce, while bird song surrounds us.

Later we walk across the deserted courtyard to
long stone barns, as she unlocks heavy doors
we enter an enchanted space.

Scenes of art unlimited, as canvas piled on canvas
lying against each other as though asleep,
uncounted but probably in their thousands.

These large barn-spaces are like a treasure house
full of nudes, portraits, still life; a wondrous riot
of brushwork with line, colour and texture.

She uses space and light to capture the essence
of people and objects with a confident eye
and an exuberant love of life.

Before we leave this humble lady surrounded by
her memories and her art, an unexpected
request is made; who could refuse?

Romi sketches us.

Gone Home

They said 'A peaceful death' maybe it was

but not for those he left behind,

should we have known

it was just a 'going home'?

Not dead, so cold and hard

but into warmth,

the welcome from a joyous throng

of those who know the truth,

that he had never really left;

Only the body, a shell, cocoon –

but all that was within, the life

the laughter, joys and griefs

live on, with you.

At Sea.

A jagged explosion of light flickers
on the horizon
storm clouds menace the ship
as she ploughs
her way through broken waves
and growing swell.

A storm petrel flies low to the water
skimming the waves. The ship dips and rises as
the horizon plays hide and seek
and passengers feel sick.
Inside we sway from side to side,
hang tight to rails where paper bags
flutter like flags in a gentle breeze.
The storm-god's rage subsides.

A Meditation after Reading Psalm 65

Silence reaching out into eternity
     silence bounded by eternity
silence speaking volumes.
      Into silence hearts sing
praise.
Praises purchased out of heart's obedience,
     prepared as a prayer
 gifted by Love.

Plastic

Sitting on the park bench one windy day
eating my lunch, cheese sarnies
milky bar, a few grapes and water,
when a gust of wind snatches
the bag from my hand.

The white plastic bag is blown into a tree
hooked on a branch,
the torn tatters fluttering like leaves
or a kite flying high in the sky.

The bag hangs there for weeks,
months perhaps, till one night
a storm blows up, and with a crack and rustle
jerks loose, flies free.

Now my carrier bag is gutted
into smaller and smaller pieces,
tiny pellets of plastic ingested by fish ----
silent killer on my dish.

Saving the Planet from Plastic

Did you know that 1 mile of road can contain
6 tons of recycled plastic?
That plastic threads can be spun into textiles
or used for carpet manufacturing
and structural engineering products?
Reduce, recycle and reuse is the mantra.
Still plastic, it is indestructible.

Did you know when sea turtles ingest plastic
they die a slow painful death?
Sealions wrapped in plastic straps are
immobilized and drowned.
From sperm whales to the smallest life form
marine life is poisoned from 13 million tonnes
of dumped plastic each year.

Ditch the disposables, clean it up
is the new mantra.
New technologies are in the pipe line, scientists
wrestling with new ideas for eco-friendly products.

Methane from farms, landfills and sewage plants,
while shrimp shells and plastic-eating mushrooms
are sources for next-generation plastic.
Biodegradable.

Sound the trumpets. Roll out the bunting!
This could be the beginning of the end of plastic.

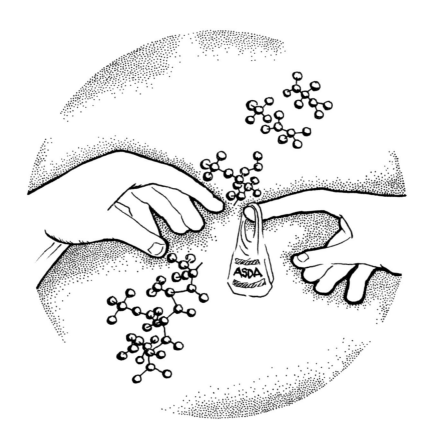

Waters

Where the River Frome meanders
through the town,
under bridges bulging and burdened
with weighty buildings,
people stop and gaze into waters
muddied by last night's rain,
while on their way to shops and cafes,
the busy daily round again.

In Wells the limpid waters wind round ancient walls
where swans glide, ducks paddle and fish
fragile as lost dreams glitter in the sun's last rays.
Here children released from school play
while workers walking home pause,
allowing the beauty of clear waters , stately trees,
and peaceful quiet to rest their weary souls.

A Morning at a Shopping Mall

He sat there isolated, alone
in that vast space of busy shoppers.
Stiff and upright, his small body
tight with tension longing for his share.

In that vast place busy with shoppers
his pale face shone out like a beacon
tight with tension, longing for someone to care.
Was he ignored by those sitting near?

His face caught my eye, I stop and stare
his vulnerability plain to see,
this child in the buggy ignored by
the girls as they shared their snacks.

His vulnerability is plainly seen
his body too thin for the cast-off clothing.
She shared her snacks with someone else
then lit a fag, laughed at a joke.

I saw him in those cast-off clothes
smoke wreathing round his head
from the fag she lit as she laughed,
his eyes pleading, asking for love.

The small boy sat there alone

A Life Long Gone

Tunnel vision grips me
   as I look down long years,
      sunny days all
   spent with laughter, joyfully
      running through meadows,
         long grass brushing my legs.
Punting down the Cam
   trailing fingers in the water
      while Flax our puppy snuffled
   a leaf he'd picked up as
      we drifted along
         in the evening mist.
I remember times in Kings chapel
   with Ruben's glorious Adoration
      shining for us, as
   organist played such music
      to set our souls alight
         on those fine nights.
I remember our first child born through
   hours of agony, my body cut and bloodied;
      yet she was perfect.
   The early years of love that flowered
      through three lives, then four
         but foundered on the rocks.
I shall not remember more.

The Windsor Chair

You are hard yet shaped
to be so comfortable that you fit
me like a well-worn glove.

What lovely woods were used
to join your parts together? Sturdy oak
elm, beech, rosewood or mahogany?

A thing of beauty glowing with a warmth of
colour
fashioned by loving hands, no iron nails used
instead some wooden pegs.

You were a gift passed
down the generations, beguiling the eye
admired by all.

Now I see you standing proud beside the
window
waiting for the next weary lover.

To the House Martin

Soaring and somersaulting

twisting and turning

scribing the sky

with windless whirls

and curving curls.

Their aerial acrobatics,

such joyous freedom in flight

proscribed only by nature's night.

A yearly welcome and a yearly mess,

houses and apartment blocks

now hold their nests.

I look up and wonder

how so small and with what food

they feed their ever-growing brood

and leave to me such moulder!

Sennen Cove

Multiple shades of blue rolling in with
gentle roars of white-capped waves breaking, dissolving
on wide curved beach.

It's early, sun rising on far horizon
heralding a new dawn. The sand is velvet
smooth beneath my feet

as cold ripples and waves' spume break.
Salt in the air tastes so good on the tongue
I lick my lips.

Grains of sand between the toes clings
to moist skin, then icy water
washes all clean.

Bathed in the shining of sun and sea
I watch as surfers slip through waves and children explore
the weed-wracked pools.

Here at the end of land, with horizon
stretching from St Just to Isles of Scilly, light planes drone
on endless journeys.

The days flow endlessly into each other. Time stops
as sun, sea and sand merge in tune to an endless
rhythm of ocean's ebb and flow.

Nora

She did for me with the first pluck
like a small tug at my heart as
she pulled on my coat to gain attention.
I turned to see this tiny lady, frail as a bird,
clothed in charity cast-offs colourful and bright,
her lovely wrinkled face shone, and I was captured.

Through weeks, months, years I watched and learnt.
 I grew to know and love her; no respecter of persons
she had no fear of men, nor any idea that people
might laugh or despise her. She walked the path
set before her, faithful and true to the call –
loving to all she met, seeing no distinction
just chatting them up, telling of her love for Jesus,
smiling gently, God's love shining out of her face.
Who could turn away? Not I.

I left long ago, moving cross-country
to Yorkshire's wilds – caught up in the small
details of a busy life. Who was she this special woman
whose bond with me lives on?
She came into my life like a breath of grace.
There was a death wasn't there? I was bereft.

Cape Cornwall

These men toiled long hours
underground in the deep dark;
dark so thick it could almost be touched.
Hour by hour, day after day they tunnelled
through granite and released the tin.
Cordite stench and earth's heated core
burnt throat and eyes, while
drills deep noise vibrated veins
and pumps sucked water to the surface.
Dynamite set, detonators fired.
Fear froze them as rocks tumbled
into their tunnel's stretch.

Exhausted by day's work they climbed
long ladders towards the light.
Men shrouded in sweat and dust returned
to the world
of crashing waves, bleak cliffs and silent moor.
Speak softly over their graves, their stones half lost
amongst encroaching grass.
Singing songs of remembrance of hard labour
and brave deeds.
Of men whose toil supplied the Empire's tin.

We sit on tufted grass, windblown
sea thrift around our feet.
Gazing out to Brison Rocks where
waves smash into monolithic blocks.
Our eyes search vainly for a sight
of dolphins or basking sharks,
while ears strain to catch the chough's
chee-ow chee-ow
or the pippit's thin cry.

Attraction

We met by moonlight

at the edges of the world.

I was blown apart by

the darkness of your art.

The squish of your ruby lips

the iridescence of your skin

against mine.

A dark fire led me to the edge

of something new.

Then I saw

through your yellow eyes

rimmed like melon-flesh,

the ending of this life

now, in thrall to you.

Daisy Days

I looked forward to those days

when we set off at dawn,

driving through the early mist

rising from the water meadows,

like pale curtains unveiling the stark outlines

of hills and valleys

unfolding before us like pages in a treasured book.

Until at last we turned the corner

saw lying before us at the meeting of sky and sea

the golden wonder of the rising sun.

Logos

By a word He formed
    all that is.
Ex nihilo He made
    the universe, and all that is
 is His.

Through the Word He came
    from above,
God became man,
    flesh of his flesh rejected
his love.

    In His word He lives
yet
    Saviour of the world
triumphant love
    has conquered death.

Journey's End

I move through St Pancras, the glassed tunnel
a busy space, heaving with figures
merging, parting, setting out on journeys
unfolding through country's furrowed fields.
I join the train, wait as it gobbles miles, for I must go
in silent expectation for the fall of shadows.

Sun shines in mid-afternoon throwing long shadows
from row on row of white standing stones; as we walk through tunnels
where sorrows ebb and flow, drawn on I go
seeing in my mind those young boy-figures,
who trudged wearily through cloying mud-filled fields
with smell of rotting corpses, their end of journeys.

I'm with my grandad on this his journey,
through trenches where rats threw long shadows
and ghosts of friends long gone still haunt these fields.
I grope my way through winding tunnels
round dark corners where bent figures
loom in eerie light surprising me, go on, I'm urged go

on for there's no end to madness in this damned place. Soldier go,
go on to face the bullets raking fire, there is no journey's
end, till Generals with their awful gaze turn figures
into faces, and see amidst the shadows
their own boys, disappearing down tunnel's
mouth with brave smiles and hand-waves, to everlasting fields.

Gas! Gas, boys! Their voices echo through the fields
as onward, forward, still they go -----
toward the green miasma, gas drifting through those tunnels
where none escape its deadly journey.
A fumbling, cursing grab at masks, for some too late, the shadows
lie in wait for those last tragic figures.

And I shall see in nightmares yet to come, those ghastly figures
cursing their unhappy lot, as through some desolate field
they slip and fall, and rise at last to raining bullets and shadowed
ghosts that claim their own. Memories tug at me to go
with him whose hopes and dreams live on. My journey
to write how he endured, bloodied but unbowed through that long tunnel.

Now drawn towards the Menin Gate I see, through tunnel
vision, long flights of stairs with rows of poppy wreaths, whose journeys
speak of nameless ones who came but unlike me, could never go.

Tyne Cot Cemetery, near Ypres, Belgium.